THE NEW YOU

THE NEW YOU

A 30-Day Motivational Guide for Making a Positive
Impact Every Day

YUSHAU SHUAIBU KATANGA

Cover design: Name of Graphic artist

Published in Nigeria by:
Words Rhymes & Rhythm
Authorpedia Publishers
Abuja | Lagos | Ibadan
08169027757, 08060109295
www.authorpedia.net

Contents

Dedication

This book is dedicated to people around the world, especially the young generation.

This book is also dedicated to my grandma, Hajiya Talata, who passed away in 2019. Hajiya Talata taught me wisdom and patience; she always spoke good words to people and always gave to charity. She was a wonderful woman who believed in living a great life and completed everything she did with goodness.

Acknowledgments

Firstly, I want to thank God for giving me the opportunity, wisdom, and talent to write this motivational book. The book was inspired by the sorrow of losing something, but God's strength to rebuild and change lies within everyone.

I also thank my family and friends for the support and courage they gave me on this journey to become a published author: My dad, Shuaibu Katanga; My step dads, Maifulani Katanga and Bello Katanga; my brothers, Dr Sufiyanu, Gaddafi Gee, and Fahad Mk. You all mean everything to me.

Lastly, my thanks go to Muh'd Mankas and Marquis hill, ale Lawan for encouraging me to write this book. They pushed me to pen down what I wanted others to know.

Thank you.

Author's Note

Dear Reader,

This book means a lot to me. Writing and publishing it wasn't an easy journey; it required much sacrifice, but it was worth it at the end.

The New You shares my hitherto hidden talent and experiences with the world. For so many years I have hidden them, but I now release them into the world in this book.

I wrote this book to motivate and provide strength for facing life's changes every day. Therefore, my message to you is this: **no matter what happens in your life, you are a new you every day**.

Use the personal notes section at the end to write down the important points you would like to pay further attention to. This will help you keep track of your progress.

Thank you reading my words, and I hope they will help you find the new *You*!

Yushau Shuaibu Katanga
December, 2021

Foreword

The New You is a collection of swarming pages; a recollection of life and self-reflection and elegant mixture of powerful ingredients designed to make a new and better you. Forged like an iron from the fire of determination, it helps the reader attain a new sense of what it means to dream, to fail and achieve.

The author gifts us a mirror that allows us to see ourselves in a new light, to study the curves and bends we are meant to straighten in our everyday lives, and to have hope in every breath and unleash ourselves into the world.

Birthed from experience, these pages carry us through the waters of fear and anxiety and deliver us onto the safe shores of success and fulfillment.

Facing Life's Problems

There are so many challenges you will face in life. They are inevitable. But, you must not let them break your spirit because, no matter what happens, there are always many paths open before us every day.

Life and problems is like the rolling dice. There are many faces and one of them must certainly turn up when the dice stops rolling. So set your mind to face whatever may turn up and be free from the needless worrying.

Surviving Life's Pain

It is important to understand that pain is a part of life; it is something that everybody feels from time to time.

Thankfully, pain is temporary.

So don't cage your life **permanently** because of **momentary** pain. Instead, focus on the many important things you have to do in your everyday life and the pain will ebb away.

Winning Life's Struggles

No challenge or struggle is too great to overcome as long as you ignore anything that tries to makes you feel inadequate. You are more than enough to win!

The real struggle is the determination that you must put in your heart so that nobody will succeed in breaking you. It is the will to keep grinding everyday till you become who you want to be. This is how you become a warrior; those who survive the war are warriors.

Find Self-Courage

If you truly want to accomplish your dreams, you must put it in your heart and keep working towards it day by day with courage. Your heart is strong and powerful. Nothing will break it or stop it from shining light into your darkness.

It is your time. Be courageous. Never let fear of failure or losing lead your day because, in life, there is no success without failure. You have a chance to keep trying and an opportunity to keep creating every day. So do everything you want to do and go after everything you want to have in your life with the self-courage to achieve.

There is Power in You

If you want to succeed as bad as you want to breathe, then you will be successful. Only by being intended on delivery can you become the best. All you need is within you.

A lion's heart is in you; beast mode is in you. Therefore, you have the power to be 100% successful in your life. If you are feeling satisfied with achieving 10% or 20% progress, I charge you to gear up and be ready to go for 100% because you have the ability.

Never Give Up

Create your own motivation for yourself. It is not easy to keep doing what you are doing every day, but you have to say 'No!' to your weaknesses and say 'Yes!' to your courage. With the *never-give-up* mindset, you can work hard (and smart) for long without retiring because you never tired until you are done with the task at hand.

Don't Quit Now

Why do you want to quit after doing so much for so many years? You have gone this far, don't quit. You are about to get to the end. Energize yourself every day because what you have been doing for many years will soon transform into a phenomenon. Remember that the path to any destination worth reaching is never perfect or easy to follow.

Keep Pushing On

Your life may be in a difficult state at the moment, but you must keep pushing on. Life presents us different situations that require us to go through both happy and difficult moments. It is during those difficult moments that you have to keep going on while constantly reminding yourself that challenges are temporary and no condition is permanent.

Scared To Lose?

You are not alone. Everyone has one fear of another fear in his or her soul. Losing is not the end, but that does not mean if it's nothing to lose something. Losing is not good, but we have to convince ourselves to take another step forward and try again, not to stop trying after every loss. It is like falling down while climbing a ladder to reach a goal and then refusing to try again. No, you have to keep trying to climb to the top again and again. So don't be scared if you lose or fall: just keep climbing until you reach to the top.

Accept Your Challenges

In life, challenges come before accomplishment and there are no challenges, there is nothing to gain. You have to accept all your challenges, defeat them and become a survivor, if you are interested in attaining success in life. You must face the challenges head-on and win or succumb to fear and risk becoming nobody.

Dominate Your Day

If you ever want to achieve anything, don't be a participant. Be the hero of your day, every day. Let each day see the real you.

Do not be like the people who just live their days without meaning, without purpose, without drive. Don't be like them! Dominate your day and make every second meaningful and you will to find pride in your life.

Value Your Day

Nobody will value your day, or your time, if you don't first show that you value it. Similarly, you will achieve nothing on any day that you do not bring the real you to the table.

If you want to attain greatness, show up to each day with the real you. Look beyond the pains, struggles, and issues, and focus on what you expect to achieve from the day.

Change Your Life

Have you recently passed through trying circumstances and problems in your life? If so, don't worry about it too much. What is past is already gone. What is left is the chance to CHANGE and create a new you. Every new day of your life means everything: you must not let anything that it is already gone hamper your future. Stay focused: you still have all the days of your life to change and renew.

Dealing With Bad Days...

You may have suffered a lot and had too many bad days in your life, but that does not mean you will not have better days anymore. It is just life happening: we have good days and we have bad days. Interestingly, it is often your bad days that will help you to evolve into the best version of yourself and create the best life for yourself.

15

Hold On To Your Faith

With faith, everything is possible…

It is a fact that many different things, good or bad, can happen in life. Despite this uncertainty, those who want to live a fulfilled and phenomenal life can do so by changing their thinking and working with faith as do the things they want to do.

You have the ability to create happiness in your life: faith will make you strong and give you courage for everything in life. Above all, faith will give you hope… and that is all you need.

Free Up Your Mind

Do not occupy your mind with worrying because you haven't gotten what you are dreaming to have. It is not an insurmountable problem because – as long as you are alive – you will have many more chances to achieve that important goal.

So always free your mind to focus on the things you can do to have what you want to have in your life. Remember (as we noted earlier) that, in life, you can win and you can lose. Losing once (or several times) does not mean you can't win again; it means you should **try again**.

Keep going with a free mind and a winning mindset with the assurance that Life will always give you another chance undo your fails.

Take Your Opportunities

Never take for granted any opportunity to do/achieve something in your life because grabbing opportunities when they come is essential if must have a successful life.

Every new day offers you opportunities to pursue (or reset) your goals. You can reset your losses in the success process by taking the opportunities that abound in our everyday life. So, take your daily opportunity to start again, activate your rebuilding power and recover all that you may have lost.

Cultivate Your Patience

As human beings, interdependent and interrelated, patience is important in our lives: in everything and in every situation. Since you cannot do all alone, you must be patient with your goals, your journey, your success, and, most importantly, the people around you.

Don't block your day with impatience, probably because of your many problems. Have patience and it will empower you to overcome any thing and achieve everything. Keep being patient and focused on achieving the things which are most important to you.

Work Out Your Success

Success is for anyone who is willing to put in the work every single day. In other words, your level of success depends largely on your level of hard (and smart) work.

You can win everything in your life and live a life of success. However, the hard truth is that you may have to endure a long period of hard work, suffering, sorrowing, failures and daunting circumstances, before you become successful.

Keep grinding because you are on the right path and, after the struggle, success will come.

Guard Your Happiness

Fun fact: Your happiness in your life.

The state of your mind – whether you are happy or sad – can determine everything in your day (or your life). So don't let your day be in darkness because of unhappiness. Light up your day by focusing on the things that make you happy and avoiding the things that tamper with your happiness.

Take note that wearing worry over your happiness will not make your problems go away. In fact, problems and worries are never-ending. Focusing on them will limit your ability to achieve anything in your day. So, choose happiness each day of your your life.

Amplify Your Joyful Days

In life, there will be both days of joy and days of sorrow. The trick in living a fulfilled and happy life, despite this unpredictable mix of joy and sorrow, is to amplify your joyful days.

Whenever you experience a day that brings you a lot of joy, ensure you enjoy it to the fullest. Bask in it: push aside every sorrow and negative things that have happened and focus on what is giving you joy. This strategy can help you survive sorrowful days with less pain.

Your Past Means Nothing

You will achieve anything in life if you keep letting what has already gone wrong in your life dictate everything you do now.

The PAST has already PASSED. So, even though wrong choices decisions made in past circumstances may have consequences, you shouldn't let them ruin everything else in your life. Put hope, and peace in your heart and start living you're a new life free of the past's chains.

Every day is a new you! Create your new phenomenal life with each new day, knowing that everything in the past has already passed and you have many more days left in your life.

Life Is Not Over

Sometimes…

1. The most uncomfortable past may lead you to the most beautiful place, and
2. Losing what you have settled for may remind you of (and lead you to) what you actually need and deserve.

A few failures, mistakes, tragedies etc. do not mean your life is over. You may never understand why are going through what you are going through until you see the new change it will bring in your life.

So, instead of acting like your life is over, value the lessons in the circumstances you been (or are passing) through and you will gain something which may not have thought you deserve or could achieve in your life.

Don't Hold Yourself Back

Never hold yourself back, whether through regret, lack of self-belief or fear of failure.

Unfortunately, you are only your enemy, if you keep holding yourself back from taking opportunities, having a second chance or making a big move, because of your past experiences. This is a big challenge because your SELF is the hardest enemy to defeat.

What has gone is not coming back so don't hold yourself down cause you will be down for good? Instead, remind yourself that life has many other paths to offer and keep going on.

Believe In Yourself

Everything will be possible in your life if you believe in yourself. Self-belief is essential. You have to believe in yourself that you can and will do everything you want to do.

Never let the pain or fear break you down and never let discouraging words keep you from your goals. No matter how hard a goal is, you will achieve it if you believe you can.

Know You Are Unique

You are a unique. There is only one YOU in this life and nobody is the same as you. Like everyone else, you are different and you have unique ways of doing anything.

If you accept this truth, that are unique and special, then you should also know that you have the ability to create, build or achieve anything. Also, you can recreate, rebuild or re-achieve whatever you have lost in your life.

Use Your Gifts

You have a gift(s); it is a unique power that can create opportunities for you to become an achiever in life. However, your gift is only a potential until you use it.

Apply your gift to your tasks, assignments and goals and you will discover that it is a key opening doors before you. Your gift will take you to your destination; your gift will allow you to achieve your dreams; your gift will make a path for you to your success...if you use it.

Conquer Your Challenges

Sometimes, before we achieve, we have to face many challenges. These challenges are part of the process and a prerequisite to success.

Do not stop in the face of challenges because challenges are meant be conquered, not surrendered to. Don't quit. Don't worry about the pressure. Keep going. With perseverance, you can have that thing you want so much. The pain will not break you. This too shall pass.

Activate Positive Thinking

Try to have a positive thought concerning all things and at all times because negative thoughts, once given a chance to occupy your mind and direct your thinking, can destroy all you have worked for. Always think wisely, and positively, before taking important decisions.

Yes, you may have a lot of problems troubling your head, but that doesn't mean you should not approach them with a positive mindset. In fact, it is in very challenging situations that you must strive the most to be positive.

With a positive mindset, you will always have the hope you need to go and do what needs to be done. So change your thinking and your life will lead you to the success you deserve.

Focus On Your Future

Let go of your past pain and struggles, not because they were not important, but because you need to focus on making your future. Yes, you have been through trying circumstances, lived in pain, endured sorrows, and survived struggles. But you must leave the past behind so you can focus on your future.

Let the past die. Live anew. The time for all the locked doors to open for you will come Focus on the future. Everything good will come.

31

33

35

37

www.ingramcontent.com/pod-product-compliance
Lightning Source LLC
Chambersburg PA
CBHW030413160726
47992CB00007B/3092